_____ WINTER LIGHT
poems by Maria Gillan

Cover Design: Kevin Hollingsworth

Acknowledgements and thanks are given to the following literary journals and anthologies in which many of these poems appeared, including *Bergen Poets 8 & 9, The Croton Review, Earth's Daughters, Free Inquiry, Italian-American Women Writers* (Schoken, 1985), *Lips, North Dakota Quarterly, Oro Madre, Sri Chinmoy Award Anthology,* 1982, 83, 84; *Visions, Writers Choice Anthology,* 1985.

© 1985 MARIA GILLAN.
All rights reserved. No part of this book may be reproduced in any form, electronic or mechnical, without permission in writing from the publisher and author.

Library of Congress Cataloging in Publication Data

Gillan, Maria M.
   Winter light.

   I. Title.
PS3557.I375W5 1985   811'.54   85-22364
ISBN 0-941608-05-0

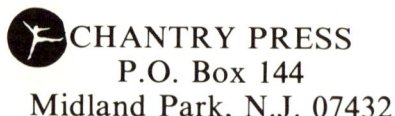

CHANTRY PRESS
P.O. Box 144
Midland Park, N.J. 07432

WINTER LIGHT	7
MY DAUGHTER AT 14: CHRISTMAS DANCE, 1981	8
LINES ON SEEING THE EYES OF SAINT FRANCIS FILL WITH COMPASSION	9
LETTER TO MY SON	11
THE PAPER DOLLS	12
PUBLIC SCHOOL NO. 18: PATERSON, NEW JERSEY	14
JENNIFER	16
AWAKENING	17
LETTER TO MY MOTHER: PAST DUE	18
DECEMBER MORNING	20
STONEHENGE LANDSCAPE	21
THE SHADOW RUSHING TO MEET US	22
CONDITIONS	24
DECEMBER DUSK	26
TO ZIO GUILLERMO: IN MEMORIUM	27
MARRIAGE LINES	28
INSIGHT ON A SUBURBAN TUESDAY	29
IMAGE IN A CURVED GLASS	30
THE ONION	32
LONELINESS	33
POEM TO JOHN: FRESHMAN YEAR, DREW UNIVERSITY, 1983	34
THE KEY TO THE GARDEN DOOR	36
THE WOMEN SPEAK OF GOD	37
MY MIRROR TO WALT WHITMAN	38
EULOGY TO BLASBERG'S FARM	39
HIEROGLYPHICS	40
THE LEGACY	41
RETROSPECTIVE	43
MA, THIS POEM IS FOR YOU	44
POEM TO MY SISTER	45
WAITING FOR THE RESULTS OF A PREGNANCY TEST	46
EBBA DAWSON: MARDEL REST HOME, HASKELL, NEW JERSEY	48

TO MY DAUGHTER AT 17	49
TO JENNIFER: WITH LOVE	50
VISION AT BARNEGAT LIGHT, LONG BEACH ISLAND, NEW JERSEY	51
STEREOPTICON	53
IN NEW JERSEY ONCE	54
SEPTEMBER LESSONS	55
A WOMAN'S VISION: EPIPHANY	56
MONDAY NIGHT VISION	58
THE PLANTING	59
WORLD OF GLASS	60
EPIPHANY	61
MORNING PRAYER	62
DAWN	63
REVELATION	64
CONVERSION	65
CONTINUITIES	66
MOMENT IN A FIELD AT OMEGA	67
MORNING IN NEW JERSEY	68
OAK PLACE MUSINGS	69
MAY MORNING	71
About the Poet	72

WINTER LIGHT

WINTER LIGHT

I have learned the litany of my life,
the pattern of repetitions orders
and imprisons.

    I have learned more than I ever
wanted to know, dream
          back into innocence,
life clean of regret and the sky
    not darkened

    yet today reels me in and what remains,
a crumb on a platter   a snow-
covered roof   pale winter light
is cause for celebration.

Even my bitter mouth
    cannot ask for more than this
my heart beating   in its cage
    my hands unclenching.

MY DAUGHTER AT 14:
CHRISTMAS DANCE, 1981

Panic in your face, you write questions
to ask him. When he arrives,
you are serene, your fear
unbetrayed. How unlike me you are.

After the dance,
I see your happiness; he holds
your hand. Though you barely speak,
your body pulses messages I can read

all too well. He kisses you goodnight,
his body moving toward yours, and yours
responding. I am frightened, guard my
tongue for fear my mother will pop out

of my mouth. "He is not shy." You giggle,
a little girl again, but you tell me he
kissed you on the dance floor. "Once?"
I ask. "No, a lot."

We ride through rain-shining 1 a.m.
streets. I bite back words which long
to be said, knowing I must not shatter your
moment, fragile as a spun-glass bird,

you, the moment, poised on the edge of
flight, and I, on the ground, afraid.

1980

LINES ON SEEING THE EYES OF SAINT FRANCIS FILL WITH COMPASSION
to Al Bennett

1.

In the sorrow of paper clips and pencils,
in the rain of forms to be filled out, sorted
and filed, in the clatter of telephones,
the hum and screech of human voices,

I have forgotten my name. Caught by my own
    compulsions,
I run through a maze of days
blurred in their sameness, trying to find
in words written in spiral notebooks,
words scrawled in the midnight kitchen,
the shape, the texture, the sound of my name.

2.

The world moves toward me.
Fear roots deep in my heart.
Through gray waves of emptiness,
I navigate the day
like a drunken schoolboy
singing brave songs to keep out the dark.
At last, I believe. If I could remember my name,
I would find salvation.

3.

Who am I to sing songs as old as time itself?
Who am I, a willing prisoner,
a minstral without a tongue,
a poor crazed thing?

In shadow, I see my face,
worn as an old woman's,
the bells of yesterday
clearer to me than today.
My hands rest empty and open.
Nothing fills them.
But my heart, that greedy traveller,
stops and starts, clutching hope
like the grail.

1984

LETTER TO MY SON

The weeks tumble over themselves
since you've been gone. The leaves
fall from the oaks.
The air turns damp and biting,
The sky gray as an old blanket.

We are unchanged, moving
in our accustomed circles.
You, miles away, have grown into a man
I can be proud of; but when you call,
I feel I am speaking to a person
hidden behind a screen. I remember

you as a little boy, your legs chunky,
your eyes gray and dreamy as a Turner
landscape. A figure moves toward you,
a younger version of myself.
She holds your hand. You speak.

Other scenes appear. She stands
at the bottom of the stairs,
calls "In a minute, in a minute,"
till your eyes close in sleep.

The weeks go by.
You spin your life into shape.
Now it is you who chant,
"In a minute, in a minute,"
and I who taste salt on my tongue.

THE PAPER DOLLS
To My Sister Laura

Darked-eyed Julio laughed his way
into our house, swung me in air.
He said: "This one is my girl"
and "I'll wait for you. Will you marry me?"

I held my mother's hand
when he married.
I never looked at his bride
or said their names.
On the way out of the church,
past confetti and congratulations,
I threw up on Mrs. Gianelli's fur coat.
She never forgave me.

We ate fresh snow with espresso on it,
sugar sprinkled on top. Nothing since
has tasted so good.

Your breasts grew first.
You were older, destined for 36 D.
I wondered why you weren't ashamed.
My own grew round as oranges, then stopped.
I was glad.

No matter what you did, men grabbed
at you, cornered you in hallways
and kitchens, thought your breasts
were a sign, wanted to drink,
to unsnap your bra.

I followed you everywhere.
We rode in Carmela's old Ford
through Bergen County dreaming.

Dreaming the lovely houses were ours,
dreaming a prince would save us.

Now in your September kitchen, I watch you
twist your hands. We are close
though we rarely speak. Those rides
in summer and winter, hopes that beat
like caged birds in our hearts,
remain stored in boxes, the lids
never open. Your body is twisted by disease;
mine bends forward as though I wait for blows.

Once I envied your breasts
as you envied my poems.
Life has flattened us both out,
turned us into cardboard figures
like our paper dolls
stiff and easily torn.

1984

PUBLIC SCHOOL NO. 18: PATERSON, NEW JERSEY

Miss Wilson's eyes, opaque
as blue glass, fix on me:
"We must speak English.
We're in America now."
I want to say, "I am American,
but the evidence is stacked against me.

My mother scrubs my scalp raw, wraps
my shining hair in white rags
to make it curl, Miss Wilson
drags me to the window, checks my hair
for lice. My face wants to hide.

At home, my words smooth in my mouth,
I chatter and am proud. In school,
I am silent, grope for the right English
words, fear the Italian word
will sprout from my mouth like a rose,

fear the progression of teachers
in their sprigged dresses,
their Anglo-Saxon faces.

Without words, they tell me
to be ashamed.
I am.
I deny that booted country
even from myself,
want to be still
and untouchable
as these women
who teach me to hate myself.

Years later, in a white
Kansas City house,
the Pyschology professor tells me
I remind him of the Mafia leader
on the cover of TIME magazine.

My anger spits
venomous from my mouth:

I am proud of my mother,
dressed all in black,
proud of my father
with his broken tongue,
proud of the laughter
and noise of our house.

Remember me, ladies,
the silent one?
I have found my voice
and my rage will blow
your house down.

1984

JENNIFER

Under the luscent skin,
the fine bones, your mind,
fierce and sharp, bites
into questions while
your quick heart cries
for all lame things

yet you fear your beauty
is only an accident
of genes colliding.

"But when they know me,"
you say, "when they know me,
they won't like me."

Daughter, hear me.
I proclaim your loveliness,

clutching your poems
in your hand, breathing
fire, I draw closer, warm
my cold hands, want
to remember you like this,
so alive I could strike
a match off your face.

1984

AWAKENING

I wake slowly, closed against the eyes
of morning. Your pillow is still warm.
The children sleep, flushed and damp,
in their beds.

The clock ticks smoothly.
The milk glasses wait in the sink.

My mother got up early
in the frozen mornings.

My day's dawning was her
eyes and hands loving me awake.

In memory, the farina still steams.
The stove murmurs. The bread
rises sweetly in its bowl.
I am safe in a circle of love.

The oak creaks and is silent.
My rooms are still.

Listen for my heartbeat.
Am I breathing?

1980-84

LETTER TO MY MOTHER: PAST DUE

Today you tell me your mother appears
to you in dreams, but she is always
angry. "You're wrong," she screams,
"wrong." You see her as a sign;
when she visits your nights, a cloud
of catastrophe bursts on your house.

Ma, hearing you tell me about her,
I see you, for a moment, as a young
girl, caught in a mahogany frame,
a young girl in a Thirties wedding
dress with a crown of flowers in your
hair, your eyes deep and terrified,

see you leaning on the rail of that phantom
ship, waving one last goodbye, think
of you, writing to her, year after year,
sending her stilted photographs of your
children, a photo of yourself, your body
young and firm in a flowered dress.

You never saw her again.
She comes to you now only in dreams, angry she
comes. Did she, once, show her love as you
do, scolding, always scolding, yet always
there for me as no one else has ever been?

Once, twenty years ago, a young man bought
my dinner (oysters and wine and waiters
with white cloths draped over their arms),
forced his way into my room in that seedy
Baltimore hotel, insisted he would teach me
how to love, and as I struggled, you called,

asked, "What's wrong? I know something's
wrong." I didn't understand how you could
have known.

Yet even now, you train your heart on us like radar,
sensing our pain before we know it ourselves
as I train my heart on my children.

Promise me, Ma, promise to come to me in dreams,
even scolding, to come to me though I have been
   angry
with you too often, though I have asked you
to leave me alone. Come to me in dreams,
knowing I loved you
always, even when I hurled my rage in your face,
   loved you
almost as much as you loved me.

July 1982

DECEMBER MORNING

This dawn, this December morning,
the world stalks me
with its cruel gray light,

the winter trees
stretched on the wrack
of a pale sky.

Safe in my lighted shell,
the profusion of orange
yellow flowers brave

the remains of an egg
on a plate
the discarded paper cups,
the melted butter.

My insomniac hours
tick by,
my skin loosening

from brittle bones
while the skeleton

in my closet rattles
and the old leering
presence stares

through all my disguises
with its prophetic eyes
merciless as a nun's.

1981

STONEHENGE LANDSCAPE

I startle awake in the hollow dark,
stumble from bed, fleeing my private
demons, yet when I reach the night-black
hall, I am lost, all day perceptions

gone, the dark air mystifies;
if this territory is unknown, what other
avenues will assume strange turnings?

My hand searches for the wall,
which inexplicably has vanished.
I see my life, the wheeling
hours, the rage bitten in two

with a smile, the sudden leap of joy,
as just so much illusion. In moments
like this, swirled through a mystery
not of my own making, I see

clearly, how little I know, how
small a creature I am.

THE SHADOW RUSHING TO MEET US
for Jennifer

My just turned fourteen was novels
through which I dreamed my hours away, and
an innocence ferocious in its blindness.
My fourteen was Sinatra records and Billy
Eckstein's syruppy voice and long gray skirts
that stopped just short of rolled bobby socks.
My fourteen was shiny little girl hair,
no style springing curly hair.

Your fourteen is Vanderbilt jeans and
Sassoon shirts, your blonde hair
perfectly ironed into curls, your cornflower
eyes, the lids blue-shadowed, bright
as sun-beaten glass. Your woman body
sends animal signals I have not learned, even now.

Yet when I drive through the dark Allendale streets
to pick you up from the dance, in the carlight,
your face, eyes are taut, shuttered. We drop Colleen
at her house. You cry. The opaque veil in
   your eyes melts

I remember a dance, a high school dance...
I stood all night on the sidelines alone. The smile
scaled from my face like old glue. My new red blouse
and plaid skirt could not cover my nakedness
as I, standing stupidly, no longer even trying
to smile, brushed away tears

as you do now. Watching your face, pleated
with anguish, I see that my fourteen and yours
are not so far apart after all. We sit in our
kitchen, I hold you, smooth away your tears,

try to tell you how we all come to it
in the end, the brick wall, the shadow
rushing to meet us.

So it is not so bad to cry now here in my arms, safe...
a dress rehearsal for the real tears
which will come sure as rain.

1982

CONDITIONS

I sew my mouth shut
with strong thread,
too strong to ever break
through,

swallow my rage
just as I've been taught
to do, a good little woman,

I don't complain, don't
shout, see how my mouth
sewn tight with invisible

thread is spread in the shape
of a smile? Except
for my eyes,

Look at my eyes, the rage
spilling out
in sparks of black fire.

Watch it woman, you're letting
it show, letting it show.
Next we'll sew your lids shut

and paste on blue eyes
blank as a summer sky
and if that doesn't work

we'll drain all your blood,
stuff you with micro chips,
punch in the program

that will make you our own.
then. compliant as toast,
you'll be willing

to give up yourself,
   always give in,
   think first of others,

and to smile
   and smile
     and smile.

1985

DECEMBER DUSK

A precariousness steals over things
at dusk when darkness bleeds the light away
and our shadows stretch their long fingers.
Objects change then. Even the sound
of the old house changes and grows dim.

The trees' menace creeps along the floor
while fear brushes against the bones.
We draw the curtains, light the lamps;
they cannot contain it, this whisper
which curls around us. We shiver at our image
in the darkening glass, our eyelids
flutter, our blood beats
against our thin skins.

1981

TO ZIO GUILLERMO: IN MEMORIUM

I forget him for years,
his shadow kindling on sunset,
his voice gravelly, his hands,
nicotine-stained and calloused,
shaping a silver ball for me

out of cigarette papers, first
small, then layer on layer, our
days silvered, the Camels consumed,
one after the other, his hands
never free of the curling smoke,

his warm smoke smell. In the summer
evenings, his hands carve intricate
bird houses, scrolled and latticed,
and wind pointers, black birds with
whirling wings. Curls of pine

beard his feet. His eyes say
I am all he has of child, this godfather
uncle, his harridan wife shoving him
through days, his eyes mild and sad.

Though he is dead now ten years,
I see him still, rustling through
corn in our bright patchwork garden,
bending over zinnias and marigolds,
calling the birds home.

1981

MARRIAGE LINES

We lie in our double bed under separate
comforts, sink into sleep moving
away. Our lives unravel
in different directions, even as we try
to move backwards, to reach
across distances.

The years roll toward us around
a hidden curve. We catch them
in our hand, praying we will not
break, praying our years
mean something, more uncertain now
than we were at twenty of where
our hearts will lead us.

Everything changes. The words
we cannot speak sink like stones
in a pond. Long after your back
is turned, I touch your shadow.

1985

INSIGHT ON A SUBURBAN TUESDAY

We drift into middleage, our smiles benign
yet the truths too terrible to tell,
we keep locked in the hidden
cupboards of our hearts.

We have learned our lessons well;
we do not breathe too deeply, and
when we stand alone at the sink,
even our tears are silent.

1985

IMAGE IN A CURVED GLASS

Janet of the freckles and the pale white skin,
Janet of the board body and knobby knees,
I remember your eyes, round and dark as raisins,
your father, runty and plain, just like you.

In your little room, we whispered behind closed doors,
laughed into mirrors, clutched our hoped-for beauty
and ventured out into the sun. We never talked
about your grandmother dying in the room
   next to yours,
her eyes blazing, the stench permeating the hall

or your step-mother who blossomed
miraculously with child. What did you think
of as you lay in that iron bed in your lopsided little
house with its thin walls? You never said.

In your lace graduation dress stretched
tight across bud breasts, your face was plain as
   a plank wearing lank brown hair.
That summer, you moved to Pompton. I took the
   bus to visit you once
and you showed me your new house, small and
   narrow as the
Thirteeth Street one, but with a brook out back
   where we ate watermelon

dripping seeds into sweet grass. We walked
   the town's
crooked streets while you whispered that you had a
   boyfriend named Ron
and you loved him. Two years later, when my life
   had filled out
with friends and school, you came to visit. We went
   together to the

Blue Stamp Redemption Center where you turned in
  your hoarded books
for an iron and talked of plans to marry Ron and of
  waiting for his
letters though sometimes they did not come. Your
  life seemed to me
then strange as a Martian's yet even in my
  separateness, I saw your loneliness
like a rift in the sky, saw a vision of your
  Pompton house

where your stepmother gave birth interminably to
  babies who
squeezed you out until you drifted away. Even then,
  I knew you had
done it already but I did not ask. We never talked
  about the things
that mattered. The cells of thirty years have been
  brushed from my hands

yet I wonder still Did he marry you? Did you pop
  one child
after another in rented rooms? I wonder do you sit
today as I do with your children nearly grown
  looking out a window
hoping this day this day something will happen that
  will give
your life meaning?

THE ONION
>*To Robert Bly*

Shaded in layers from burnt umber to pumpkin to gold, this onion curves upward in a graceful arc, the line of a womb perhaps or the shape people draw to represent women. Curved and rounded in on itself, only one burnt orange strip of skin, frail as parchment, flaps loose, pointing down and away. The rest, layer on layer, protects its heart. I am like that, private as a bud, wound tight, circling in on itself.

We are all like that, yet peel us away, one layer at a time, and underneath, at the core, each of us with a secret to tell, burning under the bleached scalp. I hold this earth fruit in my hand. Pumpkin colored lines flow upward toward the tip, never wavering in their journey as though flowing from some hidden river. Why are we so much more than we appear to be? Touch the veined skin, the cool roundness. We cannot know its secrets. It does not murmur as a shell murmurs; it keeps to itself, wrapped in its thin skin, frail and ferocious as a sparrow. Even the stars dim watching us, our backs to the wall.

1981

LONELINESS

Loneliness waits patiently, enters a woman,
a lover content to bide his time, waits through
years of childhood where his shadow forms in
darkness of closets yet vanishes always in daylight,

waits through the turning of the body toward
womanhood, the sudden unreasoned tears, waits
through the years when we move with unknowing
grace through sunlight and the dark shadow
   whispers
only in rare moments. As the years slide away,

the shadow grows more substantial, his visits
increase,
until, when we fall into forty, he enters our bodies,
finds himself a comfortable hollow and stretches.

Conscious now of the dull rhythm of blood in
   our veins,
the uneven beat of our hearts, we hear
   the world's voice
through his ears, know that even the two of us, lying

warm, warm in this scented bed, will be,
   when morning comes,
once again separate and alone.

POEM TO JOHN:
FRESHMAN YEAR, DREW UNIVERSITY, 1983

You've been gone now four weeks
It seems like forever.
You say you'll call.
I wait near the phone
so I won't miss you.
The phone stays mute.

I feel the way I did
when I let you walk home
from kindergarden
and you were late.

Only now you're grown-up
and you're doing fine.
I'm the one who can't let go,
who can't stop trying to help you,
who can't stop

stop trying
because you're grown up
and I have to not

remind you to get your shot,
and I have to not bring you blankets
and peanut butter and potato chips
and chocolate chips cookies

and I have to keep my voice down
when I see you making the same mistakes
I made.

I sit near the phone, waiting,
needing to hear from you
but not wanting to shame you by calling.
The truth is you're more grown up
than I am, and I'll try to believe
what I know already. You'll be fine
without me. You'll be fine.

1983

THE KEY TO THE GARDEN DOOR

I think of them, the madmen,
having retreated to the walled city,
they no longer bother to peer out.
I see them, hundreds of them, thousands,
all those for whom life was too much.

For most of us, the madhouse beckons, yet
is not the answer. We learn
to balance each day, like a silver bail
on the tips of our fingers,
and what it contains, we cannot know.

We take our lives in small doses;
our eyes fixed on the moment,
we cannot drown.

1980

THE WOMEN SPEAK OF GOD

The women speak of God
as though they know him well.
He is a tame creature
they invite to tea.
He sits at their table,
his finger crooked
in just the proper way.
They congratulate themselves
on their catch, this guest
they are certain is theirs.

Watching them, a gray
mouse of doubt grows
as it feeds on me.

Yet I reach toward you, even
through this darkness, reach
knowing you are

a cataclysm,
an apocalypse
which no small,
boundaried world,
clipped and safe,
could possibly contain.

1983

MY MIRROR TO WALT WHITMAN

Crazy old man, my mirror,
you crack in my skull;
your words ripple down years.
The restless nights

seize me in frenzy.
Words storm in my head,
clamoring to be written.
The world hurls itself through space,

darkens. I raise my head,
howl my anguish against
a drizzling sky. Walt

Whitman, your shadow follows me
along night-dark streets.
The years between us
melt. I salute you

across the river of the dead,
my brother,
who dragged out of the silt
of despair that star-song,

that audacious and broken-
hearted thrush who refuses,
even now, to die.

1980

EULOGY TO BLASBERG'S FARM

We used to reach it, take our
bikes up Lynack Road, pause
at gravestones in the bramble—
bushed cemetery, stones old and
fallen, wild flowers growing over
them in tangled clumps.

We sat cross-legged on the grass,
drinking our Cokes, preparing
for a journey whose distances
we could not even begin to measure.

Up Lynack Road into the back gate
of Blasberg's, we rode the crooked
rows, drowning in scented
apples, deep and scarlet
against a lilac-colored sky.

We careened down
the road, spring flying behind
us like a cloak, unaware that one
day we would mourn the tangled
underbrush, the lost curve
of apple trees, the blue
untarnished sky.

1983

HIEROGLYPHICS

Today is my brother's birthday.
The lilacs are beginning to bloom.

I sit in the early Spring kitchen
tracing the lines on my hand.
I have not seen my brother
for a long time. Even when we meet,

we are strangers meeting as if
by accident. Yet sometimes, his eyes
fix on me. There is a message there,
if only I could learn to read it.

1984

THE LEGACY

My father saves
FDR campaign buttons,
JFK fifty cent pieces,
silver coins
from 1870 and 1892.

My father saves
photographs
of his friends
playing *bocci*
at the *Societa Cilentana*
of himself, a young man
proud in his pompadored hair.

My father saves
autograph books
from P.S. 18,
a composition paper
decorated with gold stars,
my first diary.

My father saves
letters I wrote him
twenty years ago,
a certificate I won
in fifth grade,
pages from magazines
with my first poems in them.

My father saves
our artifacts, bits
and fragments he gives back to us;
each week he passes on
another piece of forgotten past,
as though in his hands
the past turned to gold.

My father saves
a picture of us
drawn by a love
that never learned English.
It is years before we hear
the words he cannot
learn to say.

RETROSPECTIVE

I grow old,
surprise

my face in
mirrors,

its sharp lines,
its eyes
burnt-out candles.

The eyes say
I have discovered
gray bones

crumbling to ash
below

the bright promise.
Uncertain,

dispossesed, I am
brown

sparrow on winter
branch

exposed to all
winds.

MA, THIS POEM IS FOR YOU

Ma, this poem is for you
who called tonight
to tell me not to write sad poems
anymore.

So I sit here
in my kitchen
surrounded by the cabinets
you insisted I buy,
drowning in orange/gold
flowers brighter
than a peacock's eyes,

and wanting to write
a happy poem for you,
I recall a field of
buttercups
and black-eyed susans
I saw as a child,
a golden-orange field
swaying with light.

In the lens of my eye,
the field remains,
untouched.

Ma, if I could
I would give you
that field, roll
you up in it until
you are buttercup gold

and when you are
powdered with light,
I would sing for you
only happy songs,
if I could,
if only I could.

1981

POEM TO MY SISTER

We talk
    to each other
        it is

emptiness
    the movement
        of air

yet I know
    inside you
        the map of your life
is burning

    you cannot shape it
        into words
            we are strangers

still

the air
    moves
        yet there are
no words
    large enough
        to carry
the meaning
    of your life
        or mine
it blossoms
    instead
like savage flowers
    crimson blood

when we look
    behind us
        even our shadows

have
    disappeared.

1978

WAITING FOR THE RESULTS OF A PREGNANCY TEST

At 41, I am uncertain of more things
than I could have imagined twenty years ago.

Your existence or non-existence
hovers over me today. The voices
of the world my friends the liberated
women who are close to me cry
abort abort abort in unison.

Yet the voice inside me shouts

        No

shows my selfishness in its mirror
my soul's dark intent.

This neut, this merging of tiny cells
makes an explosion like comets
colliding in my ordered universe.

I want to say: I'm too old, too tired,
too caught up in trying wings so long unused,
but that voice will not be silent. It beats
in my bones, cries to be allowed to live.

I did not know the child's voice would haunt
my days and nights with its primitive insistence.

Little life, floating in your boat of cells,
I will carry you under my heart
though the arithmetic is against us both.

Today I bypass the baby departments,
the thousand reminders that come to me now.
the young women wheeling strollers through
Bradlees, the girl in the maternity shirt

which proclaims: "I'm not lonely anymore."
I want to scream, we are all born lonely,
and the child beating under our hearts
does not change that. I want to lie down
on the ugly pebbled floor of Bradlees and kick
my feet and pound my fists and make this intruder
in my life vanish.

As I stand at the checkout line, I see our years
unroll:
>	the bottles
>	midnight feedings
>	tinker toys
>	baseball games
>	PTA meetings

are boulders in my path, a mountain
of boulders I will have to climb
for you. I walk into the Spring sunlight
while my life snaps closed around me and my fear.

My friends are all my age, their children in
   high school
as mine are. I will be alone with you,
You will be born with a scowl on your face,
your hands shaking, having taken from the marrow
of my bones my own quaking.

We will rock together in this leaky boat and you
will grow into my belly like a tree.
I will love you, I know, it is only in these first
moments, while I alter the picture of my life
I had painted with such sure strokes, only in these
moments that I wish wish you were not there.

1981

EBBA DAWSON: MARDEL REST HOME, HASKELL, NEW JERSEY

Ebba sits at the window
patiently waits
for the few minutes
I give.

With her, I see the others
trapped in monastic rooms
stamped with trophies
that shout I am loved:
pictures
of grandchildren tucked
in cheap dresser mirrors
Christmas cards propped
on plastic doilies.
Outside the forsythia blooms.

Ebba balances on metal canes
down brown-carpeted stairs,
trembles as we enter the restaurant,
is pleased by Lipton tea.

I touch her hand, skin almost transluscent,
threaded with lines like fish
swimming toward the river's mouth—

the fierce blue life of veins
leaping
against all odds.

1984

TO MY DAUGHTER AT 17

Let me tell you
how life goes on,
how these tears will seem like wild flowers,
beautiful and pale in sunlight,
how these moments will grow lovely
when viewed around the curve of years.

Dark nights. Despair. All the demons
yet to haunt you. If you knew,
you would treasure your longing
sharp as a knife in your throat;
your pain, momentary, illusory,
slips into a smile I bring to you
on a platter.

I would give you life,
perfect as a pear,
the bloom on the fruit untouched,
but each moment is all we have.

I give all I can; perhaps someday,
years from now, when all that you believed
seems tarnished, you will remember
and be glad.

1985

TO JENNIFER: WITH LOVE

You turn in your sleep,
your face anguished,
worry lines prominent.
I see you as clearly
as if I were with you
in your dorm room
barren as a cell.

One of your hands hangs
over the side of the bed,
cupped as though you were pleading.
Now I bend toward your face, try,
even from this distance, to soothe you.

On Sunday in the high rise dormitory, we unpacked
your clothes, set your things out on shelves.
Your face was dreamy and hopeful.

All week your voice on the phone grows thinner
As though time were slipping backward and you were
ten again.

You turn in your sleep, trying to speak;
a murmur like a groan escapes. I try
to send messages across miles of highway,
imagine my hands smoothing your hair.

1984

VISION AT BARNEGAT LIGHT, LONG BEACH ISLAND, NEW JERSEY
to Mary Ellen, Vic, and especially, Matthew.

Light falls golden
from ledge to ledge
along sea ridges
where summer arcs
through misty air.

The horizon, broken
only by black
breakers,
wears sun

haloes. My body
turns toward the other
side of light, the long
stretch of pale sand
leading to death.

Beached without warning
on my private island, I know
under my birthday songs
and candles, I am nameless.
Even my face I lose in
mirrors. Gray waves of
doubt pass through me

though I seek in
this tremor of silence
the very being I cannot
name.

yet the gulls lift
their beauty as I breathe
with them toward skies so blue

they seem unreal. The dark
face confronting my closed lids
turns light while the voices of
your world pick up the pieces
of their broken song.

1981-82

STEREOPTICON

All the people from my past come to sit with me tonight in my bright suburban kitchen, Ma, in her rocker, holding me still, telling her stories, and Daddy like dark wine, and Laura, her laugh clear as a crystal bell, and Al, his small brown hand in mine, and Zia Louisa with her huge chocolate squares, and Zia Rosa, the nights under the grape arbor, its summer sweet smell, and Zia Amalia, the mole on her nose, her foot tapping its nervous rhythm, and Zia Christina, her chickens in the garbage while we ate farina, and all the others who crowd in on me tonight while I think of my pink bedroom, cheap pink of cheap paint, and the pipes in the bathroom and the wallpaper Ma bought, how lovely it was, and even with it up, the bathroom ugly, and the linoleum in the dining room and the sofabed for Al and crowded and Molly whose husband stopped sleeping with her when she got cancer you know where and he said she wasn't a woman anymore and she cried and cried. How they crowd in on me tonight. How rich I was, though I didn't know it then.

1981

IN NEW JERSEY ONCE

In New Jersey once, marigolds grew wild.
Fields swayed with daisies
Oaks stood tall on mountains.
Powdered butterflies graced the velvet air.

Listen. It was like that.
Before the bulldozers.
Before the cranes.
Before the cement sealed the earth.

Even the stars, which used to hang
in thick clusters in the black sky,
even the stars are dim.

Burrow under the blacktop,
under the cement, the old dark earth
is still there. Dig your hands into it,
feel it, deep, alive on your fingers,

Know that the earth breathes and pulses still.
Listen. It mourns. In New Jersey once,
flowers grew.

1980

SEPTEMBER LESSONS

Little round lady,
hard as a black shoe button,
you taught me your language,
how to love,

Today you tell me you're tired,
though last week you rebuilt
the front steps alone,
pounding through cement
with a sledgehammer, prying loose
the uneven cinder blocks,
smoothing on the new layer
of cement as if
you were frosting a cake.

"I'm old," you say
The pictures rattle in the frames.
The house shakes. You're not tired.
not old. Not you. Please, say not you.

1983

A WOMAN'S VISION: EPIPHANY

In the heart's murk,
a sea star swings
through fields
of light
where clouds tremble,

break into fish,
swimming through cobalt sky
while deep in the sea's
incredible hand, they move
as they have always moved,

through salt fire and caves
of green grace. They draw
us into old sorceries
where sea and star
tremble, and

down, down fall the walls
of paradise and the blue
flowers in the deep well
mirror
your flame's

light. The heavens
tumble to earth;
chunks of sun
and blazing
sky fall into arms

outstretched
and your love,
louder than
thunder,
splits my

world. Songs grow
thick as grass.
Words like
marigolds blaze
the world down.

1982

MONDAY NIGHT VISION

In this moment, two hours past midnight
in a kitchen lit by the glare
of flourescent light, lies can no longer be told
to the self. Faces and memory draw me in
heavy and powerful as sand on the ocean floor.
This is the moment when truth begins.
The light, pure and infinite, gives me back myself
truer to form than I want to know.

Today I wondered as my voice grew sharper,
more fractured, if I had vanished
somewhere between morning coffee
and the telephone's clang, but here,
here I grow real again, thinking of rivers
and the rain which starts just outside my window,
and the cat who leaps suddenly
and settles in my lap, purring.

1985

THE PLANTING

My fingers trace the marigold's
delicate stems, their feathery
leaves, their long, damp roots
to which dark earth clings.

The soil under my hands is
cool and blessed. I rock back
onto my heels, stare into your
sky, while joy blazes in my heart.

In these moments, you are here
in my fingers which love
as you have loved me, anchoring me
deep in this earth, this flowering
               May air.

1982

WORLD OF GLASS

In my little car, I watch
the autumn night unfold,
hear the clanking of stars
in a blackened sky, the gray
light filtered through charcoal clouds.

In my little world of glass
and metal, I rush into my life,
hurtling like a comet,
yet moments such as this,

the stark beauty, nature swirling
its robes, are the golden grains
I see first when sifting through
my past,

a beauty, twisted and dark,
reached only through
caves of despair.

1982

EPIPHANY

The dark devours
the house in its
hungry maw
while the wind
swims ferociously

Through oaks bent
and growling.
I huddle in my
solitary universe
without stars or

moon while the lion
of earth eats my air.
I sink into dark rivers
rise up

as fish rise
flashing through water
heavy with silt,
rise up
to drink rain,

wind,
blackened sky,
till you hold me
in your hand's cradle. Safe
in its warmth I
rock in
        light.

1983

MORNING PRAYER

You elude me
this green morning
as alone I confront

the hours, days of my
dry season. Can you
hear me

crying in this wild place?
Dark, dark
is this hour.

Come to me now, Lord,
in this crumbling
country.
Bring your clanging cymbals,

your strummed music,
lift me up from this earth
where dirt fills my mouth,
and in your mercy,
heal me.

1983

DAWN

Here, in the early morning,
with rain running from the
gutters, the loneliness

fits like a comfortable coat
and the quiet, familiar creakings
of the house are part of me.

I am soothed by them, the sounds and
stirrings, water in the bath,
my son's footsteps on the stairs.

The sleeves of this coat are warm
on my skin. My house of bones rests
calm and singing a music all its own.

1981

REVELATION

The sun's eye
opens my new
mornings
in silence

sweet as summer.
I bite into
this pear
of quiet,

the juicy meat
of my empty
country
where you cut

with the sharp blade
of time
the taut skin
of my pilgrim self.

At the appointed hour,
I flash toward
sun-
struck space,

wade through lakes
of silence,
ponds
of blue air

where your spirit
breathes,
and the golden fruit
satisfies my unfilled
         heart.

1982

CONVERSION

The sun, that bloody
wafer, cracks the sky,
its merciless eye

larger than the
pulsing ball
of earth,
larger than our
selves,
follows where we go,

implacable,
sure of itself,
We attempt to
turn our faces; it turns
us with its incredible
hand
burning between the
firey bush and the
burned out sea.

We struggle still.
The force of its mercy
forges us in its
fire, melting away
transgressions
and love, pitiless
as a snake,
its lidless eye.

We become prophets to a
faith we did not
wish as pine tree
fingers point us
toward the vast blue
flare of sky.

1982

CONTINUITIES

Here, between the bitter houses
and sharp gray line of sea,
I bend, fluid and easy, to touch
the sand's damp coolness,
its weight heavy in my hand,
the sound of the sea
a measured rhythm in my ears.

Though the world crumbles,
here, it does not matter.
The sky, thunderous and dark,
will continue to roil,
the sea to retreat and return.
They will outlast us all.

Come. Join me. Feed on this gray light
the hard bite of wind, the water tossing,
foam-backed, against the shore.

Come...The sea and the sky remain,
unchanging and unchanged.

1980

MOMENT IN A FIELD AT OMEGA
To Robert Bly

Under water, deep where roots begin
to grow again, light filters into crevices
and caves where no sound enters.

The reeds sway gracefully as young girls
dancing in high grass. The need to wait
drops from my shoulders soundlessly.

As my hands unclench, the water whispers
the secret I always needed to know.

1982

MORNING IN NEW JERSEY

Morning in New Jersey. Houses
and leaning oaks.

I pull this gray day toward me,
hear the insistent pulse of earth
knocking in its arched room.

I reach to touch it. My hand finds
only brown branch and misty air.

Under my fingers, I feel a movement
so slight I am not certain it is there
and a warm center as if a volcano

were burning deep underground.

1982

OAK PLACE MUSINGS

1.

On my neighbor's roof, plastic butterflies
freeze in rigid postures. Rubber ducks waddle
into trimmed evergreens; plaster cats climb
siding toward peaked roofs.

Once, in a vacant Paterson lot, I caught
a butterfly; The lot seemed huge. Daisies
grew there and marigolds and red berries
which stained our fingers. We had crepe paper
whirlers in varied colors; we spun and spun.
The whirlers were an army of insects
buzzing, till tall grass and flowers blurred.

The butterfly in my hand beat its wings
in terror. My hand stained gold.
When I let it escape it flew away fast,
and then, forgetting, it dipped and swirled
so gracefully I almost stopped breathing.

2.

By 9 each morning, Oak Place with its neat box
houses, lies still and empty. Children have vanished
into yellow camp buses, parents departed in separate
cars.

The street settles into somnolence. Its lines
and angles imprison handkerchief lawns
until even the old oaks no longer seem at home.
In my yesterdays I dreamed myself out of the old city,
imagining a world just like this one,
away from strewn garbage and houses stacked close
   as teeth.

Today I mourn tomatoes ripening in our immigrant
   gardens,
the pattern of sun on walls of old brick mills,
a time when each day opened like a morning glory.
Some days when I look at my hand, I imagine
it is still stained gold.

1985

MAY MORNING

How silent it is, this flowering,
the dance of living
as though
the earth could deny death,

despite the evidence,
proclaiming the maimed
and tormented, the hours,
bleak and frozen.

One flower, in this silken air,
is enough.

In the soft shawl
of Spring,
trees prance
in their cap of flowers;
tulips ignite.

About the Poet:

Maria Gillan, won the New Jersey State Council on the Arts Creative Writing Grant in Poetry in 1981 and 1985, the Sri Chinmoy Award, and the Walt Whitman Award. Her work was chosen as a 1985 Editor's Choice selection and also was nominated for a Pushcart Prize. She has read her work at colleges, universities, and Poetry Centers throughout the U.S.A. Her first book of poems, *Flowers From the Tree of Night,* was published by Chantry Press in 1981 and a second printing was completed in 1982.

The Editor of *Footwork* magazine, Ms. Gillan also edited, *The New Jersey Writer's Directory, The New Jersey Poetry Resource Book,* and the *Passaic County College Poetry Center Anthology.* She is the Director of the Poetry Center at Passaic County Community College, and a Ph.D. candidate at Drew University.

In addition, Ms. Gillan has taught at Drew University, Bloomfield College, Passaic County Community College, and the University of Missouri.